Survival Book
Everything You Need to Know
Before Disaster Strikes

I0411133

By Carol Marshal

Table of Contents

Introduction

Imagine, if you will, that you awaken tomorrow morning and the world is a much different place than it was when you went to sleep the night before. First, you notice that your house is unusually cold, and then you observe that your electronic clocks are flashing. As you make your way to the window, you see total darkness as the streetlights are not working and there are no cars on the road. You pick up your cell phone to call your friend, but your cell phone isn't working. You make your way out to your driveway and attempt to start your car, but that isn't working either.

The scenario described above could be caused by what is known as an electromagnetic pulse, or EMP. An EMP could be caused by a solar flare from the sun, or from the after effects of a bomb of some sort that could be detonated by one of any number of rogue countries or terrorist groups that exist today.

There are plenty of other events that could occur in our world that could totally disrupt the way we live, including natural disasters such as hurricanes, tornadoes, floods, and volcanic eruptions, as well as man-made disasters such as war, bombs, and terrorist attacks. Consider the following facts, if you will:

- Hurricane Katrina, the costliest and one of the five most deadly storms to ever hit the United States, struck in August of 2005. No one really knows how many people died during and after the hurricane, but estimates range in the 1,200 to 1,300 range. The cost of property damage exceeded $108 billion. While the storm had been predicted by meteorologists, and preparations were made by both governmental agencies and individuals, there were many errors in judgement that ended up costing many lives.

- Try as they might, the experts have great difficulty predicting earthquakes around the world and when they occur, they have the potential to do huge damage to the surrounding infrastructure including buildings, bridges, tunnels, and highways. The earthquake that occurred in central Italy in August, 2016 killed nearly three hundred people, turned the town of Amatrice to rubble and left many people homeless and without shelter.

- In September 2016, the country of North Korea continued testing of their nuclear arsenal and upped their threats against both South Korea and the United States. No one knows when, or even if, North Korea's leadership will decide to launch an attack, but the possibility is certainly there. We do know, however, that if nuclear weapons are ever used anywhere in the world again, that would pose a grave threat to civilization as we know it.

As far off and detached these scenarios may seem to you, it certainly is not outside the realm of possibility that something that threatens our current way of life could occur in our near or distant future. Our country and our world is largely dependent on our electrical grid and the technology that uses it every minute of every day. We depend on our first responders, our hospitals, and our governmental institutions to take care of us when something catastrophic occurs, but these organizations have their limitations. In the event that mass casualties take place during and following a disaster, governmental emergency services will be overwhelmed and many of us will have to fend for ourselves. Will you be ready?

You can better prepare yourself for a disaster by anticipating how you and your world will be affected when and if it happens, and then preparing accordingly. Once you have designed your disaster plan, it's just a matter of maintaining and updating it in order to keep it current. This book will help you prepare your plan, and be ready to implement it if and when it ever becomes necessary.

Chapter 1: The Prepper Movement

The prepper movement has grown significantly in the last several years, but has been around in some form since the 1930s. Its recent growth is attributed to a distrust in governmental systems, the rise of rogue states, and the threat of terrorism. These factors have led a great number of people to design and implement plans for survival in the event of either a natural or man-made disaster with catastrophic consequences.

Those who have devoted their efforts come from all walks of life and hold a wide variety of perspectives about government, politics, and religion, but they all share a belief that our world as we currently know it may drastically change at some point in the near or distant future. They also believe that if they do everything within their power to prepare for a potential calamity, they and their loved ones stand a good chance of surviving it.

Much has been written about disaster preparation, both in literature and online, and this book does not pretend to offer all of the answers people may have about the topic. Rather, this book has been written for those who are approaching the idea of disaster preparation, perhaps for the first time, and offers basic information to think about as one begins and moves into the process.

Keep in mind that disaster preparation can be a complex topic, mainly because one can never quite be sure what sort of disaster will occur. Most natural disasters such as hurricanes, tornadoes, and blizzards have the potential to do great damage, but historically, these types of events can be addressed in a way that services are generally restored in a relatively reasonable amount of time.

But what if, say, for example, a major city was hit by an earthquake that wiped out the infrastructure and a majority of the buildings in a ten-mile radius? That sort of catastrophe would most likely create much more devastating consequences and would take much more manpower, time, and money to bring things anywhere near back to normal.

It's also worth mentioning that many preppers take into account the threats that exist due to geopolitical factors, including financial and / or governmental collapse, terrorism, or nuclear war. For obvious reasons, disasters that could occur as a result of these issues cause greater concern for those who are focused on preparation because the recovery time from something like that could take years, even decades.

In this book, we focus primarily on preparing for relatively short-term disasters, although most of the topics we discuss would be helpful in a long-term situation as well. As you begin to think about preparation, we recommend taking some time to ponder the following questions:

Questions You Should Ask Yourself

Question 1: What exactly do I need to prepare for?

Research those issues that you think could be potential threats locally, nationally, and globally, and use your research to help you decide what to prepare for and how to go about doing it. Rome was not built in a day, and your entire plan does not have to be designed and implemented that quickly either. The important thing is that you have begun to prepare just by giving thought to the process, and you can build upon it from there.

Question 2: How will I defend my family and my belongings?

This is a critical question, because you can bet that not everyone will take the time to prepare for a disaster and people will most likely come to you for assistance if word gets out that you have what they need. Hopefully, they will come with things to trade with you, but some may show up with the idea that they are going to take from you.

For that reason, you need a defense plan. There is a wide diversity of opinion about how folks should defend themselves in threatening situations and you are going to have to make up your mind about how you will respond if someone gets aggressive. Whatever you decide, make sure you have what you need to implement your defense plan.

Question 3: How much food and water will I need to sustain myself and my family?

This is a challenging question because one simply cannot be sure how long it will take to restore basic food distribution services following a disaster. It's best to have plenty of nonperishable food on hand and stored appropriately. Additionally, you should store water and have a water purification plan as well. The amount you store may depend on available space and available funds.

Question 4: How can I keep the lights and the heat on?

Will you purchase a generator? If so, what type? Where will you store it? Will you consider installing a wood stove in your home? If not, what are your other alternatives? Will you combine assets with extended family or friends in order to share and conserve energy?

Question 5: What skills or goods do I need to acquire for bartering purposes?

It's best to begin to think about this question sooner than later, because you may have to hone a skill or two now in order to prepare for a disaster. There is a section in this book that discusses bartering in more detail and provides ideas for what items to have on hand to barter with others.

Question 6; How will I communicate with the world and receive information?

This is a somewhat complex question because while we hope that someone will be broadcasting following a calamity, we can't be sure that that will be the case. Perhaps you will consider investing in a ham radio and learn how to use it. If you do that, you will have a better chance at being able to communicate AND have a barterable skill as well.

Question 7: How will I pay for all of my preparations?

Obviously, disaster preparation requires some sacrifices in terms of time, energy, and money, and you are going to have to allocate resources if you are serious about preparing for a disaster.

We, of course, believe that the investment now could very well save you in the future.

Preparation Reduces Panic

Thoughtful planning for a natural disaster requires time and energy, and it all may be for naught if nothing disastrous ever happens. But it is worth considering that the time and energy you expend today on disaster preparation could save you much stress and anxiety in the future should something bad ever occur. In fact, effective disaster planning and preparation could even save the lives of you and your loved ones.

Planning takes away much of the uncertainty when one faces an emergency situation. That's why first responders regularly train for disasters, analyze their training, adjust, and train again. The better prepared you are, the less there is to fear when disaster strikes.

But training and preparation takes time and effort. One has to carefully consider what the threats are within their region, and then do the research to figure out what they need to do in order to protect themselves against those threats. Once the research is complete, then the work of designing and implementing a plan begins.

The rest of this book is broken down into various sections, and each section addresses different areas of preparation that are necessary to have in place when disaster looms. Although you are certainly welcome to read the book from cover to cover, feel free to flip right to chapters that you find interesting. Be sure to read the whole book, though, because learning and using the information provided here could keep you safe and may even save your life in the event of a disaster.

Chapter 2: Prepare Yourself

There is a really good reason flight attendants instruct adult passengers on airplanes to place their oxygen mask over their faces first and then help others do the same. This is because they cannot be any good to anyone else unless they prioritize their own survival first.

The same rule applies to anyone who plans to spearhead an effort to design and implement a plan for survival during and following a disaster. You have to address your own mental, emotional, and physical needs first before you can be good for anyone else. Mental, emotional, and physical fitness takes time and effort, but investing in these areas of your own life today will not only help you survive in times of disaster, but may also help you help others survive as well. Let's discuss each of these three areas of self-preparedness in a bit more detail

Task Number 1: Keep Yourself Mentally Fit

Life is unpredictable. For that reason, you need to be on your game. This does not mean that it is necessary to walk around your world in a paranoid state all of the time, but it does mean that you would be wise to let your guard down only when it is prudent to do so. Mental strength can be defined as knowing what to do and when to do it. You are going to need to be an effective planner, motivator, and taskmaster. In addition, you are going to have to pay attention to a lot of different variables in your world in the short term, and in the long term before, during, and following a disaster. Keep yourself sharp. Figure out what your goals are, develop a plan to reach your goals, and then work on them every day of your life.

Be smart. Be aware of what is happening globally, nationally, and locally. When you are out in the world, be aware and avoid risky areas where trouble may occur. As of this writing, there were bombings in New York City and in New Jersey and attacks in two malls in the United States in the last two weeks. No one expects these sort of attacks to happen when they go into a mall or walk down the street, but it's always best to hope for the best and be prepared for the worst. Be totally aware of your surroundings when you are out in the world. If you go into a restaurant, theater, or any other public building, make sure you know where the exits are in case you need to evacuate the area quickly.

The experts always advise us to say something if we see something out of the ordinary and this is good advice. Pay attention to bags or packages standing alone in airports, train stations, or grocery stores, for that matter. Carefully observe people who seem to be acting in ways that are strange or even slightly inappropriate for the environment in which you find yourself.

If there is no one around to notify when you see something out of the ordinary, then call 911 from your cell phone or deal with it yourself if you have the capability to do so. On September 11th, 2001, several passengers on United Airlines Flight 93 reacted quickly and ended up taking down several terrorists before they could direct that plane into the White House. It was a difficult mission for all of them, and they all probably knew that they were going to perish, but they did what they did for a greater good. The character it takes to engage in such courageous behavior is something you should strive to develop within yourself. You may well need it in times of disaster.

Of course, because we are well aware these days that trouble can occur anywhere, it is best to avoid risky behaviors that may reduce your ability to respond quickly and purposefully if something happens. Many of us like to enjoy a day or a night out on the town occasionally, but smart people will keep their senses tuned enough to pay attention to activities within their surroundings wherever they are and whenever they are away from their homes. Mental fitness requires the ability to think and act responsibly. Manage your stress levels and your emotions. Don't overindulge in alcohol, and steer clear of all illegal drugs. Keep your mind alert and active when you are out in the world and you will be safer for it.

Task Number 2: Keep Yourself Emotionally Fit

Emotional fitness can be a real challenge for a lot of people these days. Many of us can be triggered emotionally by persistent telemarketers, bad drivers, impatient customers, crying babies, and needy spouses, and then we don't know what to do with our stress. Consequently, we lash out at people, act passive-aggressively toward those who trigger us, or end up stuffing our negative feelings, which is dangerous because those emotions will often come out again in ways that are self-destructive.

It is worth remembering that your perception is your reality. In other words, the way you think about a particular situation will directly affect your reaction to it. Let's look at an example:

Imagine it is a beautiful cloudless Sunday morning and a man is driving his car in the center lane on a relatively busy highway on his way to see his friends in another town. Suddenly, he notices a car coming up very quickly in the left lane next to him and when the car passes, the driver quickly jerks his car directly in front of our friend in his lane, causing him to have to brake quickly. The reckless driver then continues into the right lane, where he causes another driver to have to brake quickly in order to avoid hitting him. Then, he speeds off.

The first driver glances over at the driver in the right line, who is yelling and screaming and speeding up in an attempt to catch up with the driver who had cut him off. The first driver, on the other hand, continues to drive safely, and chooses not to react with anger as the other driver has done. What causes one driver not to react to such a disruptive event while the other one reacts strongly?

It's all about self-talk, or what we tell ourselves in our heads in response to stressful events. The first driver, even though he was startled by the actions of the reckless driver, kept himself calm by not taking the event personally. He may have said something like this in his head in response to the event:

"That guy sure is in a hurry," or;
"That man is driving very erratically, and I am very glad he didn't hit my car."

The guy who reacted with anger or rage, on the other hand, may have responded with self-talk that might sound something like this:

"What an idiot, cutting me off that way. I'll show him!" or;

"That ass needs a taste of his own medicine and I'm going to give it to him."

Do you see the difference in these reactions? The first driver does not take the actions of the reckless driver personally, and prioritizes his own safety and mental wellbeing over the need to lash out at the bad driver. This is not to say that the first driver does not feel aggravation or anger at the bad driver; it simply means that he has chosen to perceive the incident in a way that keeps him safe from harming himself or someone else.

The second driver, on the other hand, is more easily triggered by the actions of the bad driver and chooses to take his actions personally. There are any number of reasons why people perceive events like this as personal attacks, but it is often because they are carrying unresolved anger within themselves already.

The point here is that you can actually choose how you can respond to stressful events. You can choose to do what many will do when disaster strikes and become despondent and desperate, or you can choose to act with calm and focus and get yourself through the danger with poise and confidence.

Take the time now to gain better control of your emotional management if you have not done so already. Learn the art of meditation and the benefits of mindfulness. Meditation involves spending time in a quiet place for purposes of relaxation. Mindfulness is the art of living in the moment, as opposed to focusing on the past or the future. It is about enjoying what is, and not regretting what was or worrying about what might be.

Learn to manage your anger. This can be particularly challenging, but there are plenty of resources out there to help you learn anger management. When disaster strikes, you are not going to have the time or the energy to waste on getting angry with people, places, or things. Instead, you are going to need all of your internal resources to get things done in order to survive and to help your loved ones do the same. Take care of your emotions and you will be happy that you did in the long run.

Task Number 3:   Keep Yourself Physically Fit

Keeping yourself in good physical shape is advantageous for several reasons. For one, physically fit people are generally healthier than those who do not strive to keep their bodies tuned, and you're going to find survival a lot easier if your health is satisfactory. Many studies have shown that mental and emotional stress can lead to physical stress as well, and you will be one step ahead of the game if you are as physically healthy as you can possibly be.

Another reason to strive for physical fitness is that you are most likely going to need all of the strength you are able to muster in a disaster. Those who have invested the time and the energy to develop their muscles and their bones and their tendons to the best of their ability will be better able to take care of physical issues if and when the need arises. Depending on the type of disaster you may face, it is quite likely you may experience conflict with others and have to defend yourself and your family from human or animal predators. In addition, if you have to leave your home and head for new territory, you may have to walk long distances with supplies and gear strapped to your back. The more in tune your body is for such an event, the better able you will be to do what you have to do.

Before you jump in and begin an exercise program, though, it is highly recommended that you visit your physician and get checked out to make sure you are healthy enough to do what you are planning on doing. Depending on how long it has been since you last exercised seriously, you may have to begin slowly. Don't despair, though, because with regular exercise, you will be making in progress every week.

Stamina requires a strong cardiovascular system, and for that reason it is a very good idea to build yours up to the best of your ability. Getting in shape does not have to feel like work, contrary to popular belief. It does, however, require you to get off of the couch and either walk, run, ride a bike, swim, or participate in some other activity regularly that will cause you to breathe heavily and to raise your heart rate. Start slowly, as there is absolutely no reason to place undue stress on your body prematurely. If you have not exercised for a long period of time, begin by walking for fifteen minutes three days per week, and then gradually lengthen your walk each week. Eventually, you are going to want to be able to walk briskly, or even jog, for thirty minutes each day for five days per week.

In addition to building up your cardiovascular system, focus on building your muscle mass. This is done through using resistance exercises that challenge the muscles in your arms, shoulders, back, abdomen, and legs. Many people use weights to build up their muscles, but others practice Yoga and other floor techniques that focus on using body weight for resistance. The goal is to strengthen your muscles so that you are better able to lift, push, and pull yourself through potentially stressful situations. The stronger you are, the better able you will be to take care of yourself instead of relying on those around you to help you survive.

Many people have found it very challenging to begin to get in shape by themselves, and that is why there are many organizations, both for-profit and non-profit, that you can join in order to be motivated by participating in group activities. Visit a few gyms in your area to see what they offer and what they charge, and then look for free group activities in which you can participate. If you live near the mountains, consider joining a hiking club, and if you are near the beach, check out kayaking or canoeing clubs. The point is that there are all sorts of ways to get help when you make the decision to get in shape.

Task Number 4:   Educate Yourself

Most people have no idea how to survive in the event of a disaster, but there is really no reason to remain ignorant about survival techniques. As I have previously stated and as I will state many times throughout this book, we reside in an unpredictable world and the more information we have about how to remain safe and satiated in tough times, the better our chances for survival.

This book covers a lot of general information regarding survival, but there is a lot more information available out there that goes into much more detail regarding how to prepare for disaster. If you choose, you can find a lot more information that addresses the topics of survivalist techniques and the prepper lifestyle that will help you expand your knowledge regarding how to prepare, and how to survive.

Once you have made the decision to take the time to prepare yourself and your loved ones for events that we all hope never occur, it's important to keep abreast of what's going on in the world in which you live. Thanks to the wonders of technology, it's relatively easy to follow local, national, and global activity that could potentially set up a catastrophic situation. Check in with at least one, and ideally two or three news sources each day to monitor headlines at the minimum. It is smart to monitor at least a couple of media outlets because sometimes the one you prefer may miss, or be late, on a story that could give you important information about a possible threat. Major media outlets do not usually miss important stories, but it has happened in the past, so be thorough in your news monitoring every day.

The other reason to pay attention to more than one news source is because of bias. Information dispersed by media outlets is very often skewed toward one perspective or another. While this may often be unintentional, you need to remember that media are operated by human beings and most are supported at least in part by either big business or governments. Thus, they have an agenda of some sort, and may be reporting news and news stories in a way to attempt to influence viewers' opinions in some way. This is neither good nor bad, but it is a reality of which you need to be aware as you gather your news information.

Chapter 3; Prepare Your Family

Task Number 5:   Discuss Your Preparation Plans with Your Family

Unless you are totally alone in the world, and I sincerely hope that you are not, you are most likely going to have a vested interest in assisting family members and / or friends in the event of a disaster. Let's assume that, since you are taking the time to read this book, you will take a leadership role in helping your family know what, and what not, to do when disaster strikes.

I stated in the previous section that most people have no idea how to survive when disaster strikes, and I will go further now and say that many people make the conscious choice not to take the time to learn. This is because people hate to think of bad things happening to them. It's much easier for some, in fact most, people to avoid even thinking about preparing because it's very uncomfortable to think about the end of the world as it exists today.

As you consider preparing your family, you need to think about how to talk to them about disaster prevention and preparation. Think about how you can use your communication skills to persuade them to take an active role in the process. Your goal should not be to scare them, but rather to point out the reality of what could potentially occur. Sadly, we are certainly not without examples of people being caught totally off guard when a hurricane or a tornado hit, or when the power grid went down, or when terrorists struck. Rather than spending too much time focusing on the negative, though, let them know the good news, which is that with proper planning, one's tendency to be harmed or worse can be significantly reduced by doing some strategic planning implementation now.

Let's address the issue of how to communicate the relevance of your plan to children for a moment. We can all agree that disaster planning is not easy to even think about for many people, let alone address, and it can be particularly difficult for children to comprehend. Your goal, from the time your children are old enough to think conceptually (usually around the age of five or six, according to experts), should be to talk to them about the importance of planning for emergencies and to get them involved in the process. Sadly, unless they are homeschooled, it's a fair assumption that your child has been involved in "active shooter" or other emergency drills at their school, so the concept of preparation for challenging scenarios should not be new to them.

Remember that the goal is to educate them about the importance of disaster planning, and to teach them that proper planning is a good thing that will make them stronger and more prepared to address obstacles that may get in their way at some point. Make it positive and keep it positive.

Task Number 6:   Agree on a Rendezvous Point

One of the most important things to consider when thinking about putting a plan together is to think about what could occur, and it is fairly common knowledge that electrical power can be knocked out fairly easily, even in the event of a windstorm. Because today's world is so dependent on power, a failure has the ability to cause some real hardship for many folks. Power failures can affect transportation systems and cellular service, and regular telephone service, not to mention email. For that reason, your family needs to select a place where you will all congregate in the event of a sustained emergency, and everyone has to establish a plan that will help them get there if power is down for a sustained period of time. For example, if the agreed-upon rendezvous point is your mother's house in the suburbs and you routinely take the train into the city to work five days a week, you should have at least a tentative plan to direct your efforts to get back to your mom's home if the trains are not running. Establish a route you can take on foot and keep a paper map of that route with you when you go to work. In addition, you should be familiar with several routes to your rendezvous point from all directions, because you may be somewhere other than work when disaster strikes or your direct route may be blocked for some reason.

The place you select may be your home, or the home of someone who is centrally located, and it should be a place of relative safety and should be set up with supplies that will sustain all who end up there for at least thirty days. If there are children involved in your plan, make sure that they know the address of the rendezvous point so that they can communicate it to anyone who will be available to assist them if in the event you are unable to do so.

Task Number 7:   Distribute Paper Backups of Phone Numbers, Addresses and Important Personal Documents

It was not so long ago that people used to keep address books in their homes and offices that listed the names, addresses, and phone numbers of important people in their circles. In addition, we had committed many important contacts to memory. The technological age, however, has changed all of that. We no longer keep lists or commit numbers to memory because we simply push buttons or icons on our phones that are designated for important people in our lives, which leaves all of in a jam if our cell phones suddenly do not work anymore.

This is why it is a smart practice to make sure that everyone in your family has a paper backup of all important phone numbers and addresses. You may never need it, but it may come in handy if the lights go out. Lists should be kept with you at all times, as in a wallet or another item that you always carry with you. Laminate them in order to protect them and to keep them dry, and have backups of your lists in case something happens to the originals.

Everyone in your family should also have copies of important documents such as drivers' licenses, birth certificates, and passports with them as well. This may be tedious work, but it may be well worth it in a critical situation.

Task Number 8:   Have an Evacuation Plan and Practice It

Different areas of the country experience different hazards. People who live in Florida and on the eastern seaboard have to watch for hurricanes during certain parts of the year, and others who live near nuclear power plants are hopeful that the plants are properly maintained and a meltdown will never occur. As we have stated previously, though, there is no such thing as a sure thing, and that's why communities with these sort of potential hazards have designated routes that people are encouraged to use to evacuate the area when the going gets rough.

Not only should all of your loved ones be aware of these routes, but you all should practice dry runs every now and then in order to minimize confusion and chaos if and when the day comes when you need to take flight. Keep in mind, though, that if those routes are ever needed, there is definitely going to be chaos because everyone will be trying to use them at the same time, and most people lose their minds in stressful situations. For this reason, it would be smart to seek out alternative routes that may take you off of the main roads for a spell, provided that they are safe and passable. Your stress will be significantly reduced if you take the time to practice what you will do, and where you will go, in the event of an emergency situation.

Chapter 4: Prepare Your Finances

Task Number 9:   Set Aside an Emergency Cash Fund

We all take our money for granted, but take me seriously when I tell you that the currency in this country is anything but a sure thing these days. As I write this, the United States debt sits at just below twenty trillion dollars. Here's what that number looks like in numeric form:

$20,000,000,000,000

Huge, isn't it? Economists tell us that, sooner or later, that debt will have to be paid. I am not going to cover the reasons for this mess in this book, but you can find many resources online that will provide you with much more information regarding this topic.

Keep in mind that those dollars in your pocket are worth only what others say they are worth, and the day may come when they are worth little or nothing. Or, there may come a day when banks will not open for some reason and you will not be able to access the funds you have in your bank accounts. Here are some things you can do to prepare for the unpredictable when it comes to your money:

Never keep all of your funds in one place. Those who teach money management advocate diversity for good reason: if that one place that holds your wealth goes down the tubes, you are sunk. You greatly reduce your risk of financial ruin if you invest in a variety of assets and keep your money in various accounts.

Keep a cash fund on hand and nearby. Remembering that nothing is a sure thing, even the FDIC's guarantee at banks, you should always keep a stash of cash that is readily accessible with minimal effort. The cash you keep on-hand should be enough to sustain you for at least one week or longer and should be broken down into small bills. It is advisable to keep your stashed cash in a safe of some sort to which only you and one other person has access.

Saving for a rainy day is not the easiest thing to do, given all of the obligations and temptations we are faced with on a daily basis. We are a nation heavily indebted, which has sent a message to many of us that it is okay to carry a lot of debt. We tell ourselves that we will pay off our debt when our situation improves, but that never seems to happen.

Take time as soon as possible to address your debt so that you can begin to build your savings. No matter how much you bring home from each paycheck, commit to setting aside at least a portion of your income each pay period and putting it in an account that you will not touch until you need it in an emergency.

There is no such thing as a totally safe investment, but some are definitely safer than others. Take care of your debt obligations first, and then consider investing some of your earned capital in investments that you have carefully researched and that appeal to you. Remember to diversify whatever investments you make in order to protect yourself from total loss.

Task Number 10: Buy Gold and Silver

Buy gold and silver, for they have held value throughout centuries. Hard commodities have traditionally increased in value when the value of stocks and bonds decrease. Gold has traditionally held value because it is the logical choice for making coins due to its resistance to rust and corrosion, and because it is weighty and beautiful. Silver is also valuable because it can be made into items such as coins and jewelry. In tough times when the value of paper money may decrease significantly, you will be wise to have gold, silver, or both in your possession.

When you purchase gold and silver, it is recommended that you buy coins as opposed to bars. This is recommended because coins are easier to transport in case you have to "bug out," or evacuate, and more people will be interested in trading currency that is easy to carry. There are plenty of places online where you can purchase gold and silver coins, and there are probably banks and coin shops in your local area where you may purchase silver and gold coins as well. Look for bullion coins as opposed to numismatic coins, because bullion coins are going to contain more silver or metal. Gold is much more expensive than silver and it would be wise to have a mix of both gold and silver coins in the event that paper money becomes obsolete.

Task Number 11: Design a Bartering Plan

In a worst-case scenario, all currency may become worthless and you will be forced to fend for yourself to take care of your basic needs. If this occurs, you should have some skills and items from which others may benefit so that you can trade for what you need. This is yet another reason for you to keep yourself in top physical shape, and to develop skills and talents that will be barterable when money is short or nonexistent.

By reading this book and learning about the topics discussed here, you are already on your way to building a knowledge base about survival. The information you learn here can potentially help you survive by virtue of the fact that most of the population will not have this knowledge with disaster strikes, and they will offer you things you need in exchange for your assistance or knowledge.

Like most everything else we discuss here, you can prepare for the need to barter by learning as much as you can now, and by developing a plan to share that information with others. Perhaps you could write your own e-book about one specific area related to survival, such as urban farming or cooking and preparing food over an open fire. Since electronic books may not work due to lack of power in an emergency, you may want to self-publish your work and store copies in a dry, secure area for distribution following an emergency, in exchange for goods, of course. Or, you may choose to become certified as a CPR instructor or First-Aid instructor and share that information with others in exchange for items or services you may need.

Survival skills may not only save you, but they may also be useful as you trade them for food, water, or shelter.

You may also consider stocking up on items that you may use to barter with others. There are plenty of choices. Think of what people may need, and then think of what people may want. Here is a list of items that people will need in times of crisis and may not have:

- Batteries

- Matches / lighters
- Toothbrushes / toothpaste
- Food
- Phones / phone chargers
- Fuel
- Tools
- Soap
- Toilet paper
- Water

Basically, you can stock up on anything others may need in order to survive and use them to barter for things you may need.

There is also value in items that people may not necessarily need, but that give them pleasure and relieve them of stress, at least temporarily. These items include:

- Alcohol:
- Cigarettes
- Magazines

- Gum / candy
- Coffee
- Condoms
- Games / playing cards

Whatever items you decide to offer for bartering, think about purchasing them in bulk in order to keep your costs down. Then, put items, such as cigarettes and coffee, in smaller packages so that you can sell smaller quantities for higher value. If at all possible, have enough on hand so that you always have something of value to offer for items you may need at some point.

Chapter 5: Prepare Your Food, Your Water, and Your Gear

Task Number 12: Grow Your Own Food

Humans cannot survive without food or water, and most humans rely on others to grow the food they eat and filter the water they drink. In an emergency situation, though, there may be food and water shortages, or the food and water supply may become damaged so that it is not safe to consume.

For these reasons, you must learn to grow your own food, and most survivalist experts recommend that you begin sooner than later. This makes sense because we never know when a disaster, whether man-made or natural, will occur, and it takes some time to grow the food you will need to sustain you and your family.

There are many websites and books that are devoted to growing food for survival purposes, and one of the more interesting strategies that have been written about is making sure your garden is secure. Of course, food has the ability to be a scarce commodity when chaos erupts, and one cannot be at all certain that their food source will not be stolen by those who have not taken the time to prepare for food shortages. A lot of people will end up growing their survival food within or very close to their homes, but others have opted to grow their food covertly in relatively common areas. These so-called "secret gardens" often yield a great deal of edible foods but grow virtually undetected because of the plant growth around them.

Once you figure out how and where you are going to grow your food, you will need to decide what foods to grow. Experts agree that you should concentrate your efforts on growing foods that are easy to grow and that contain an abundance of calories in order to sustain you and your family. Chances are good that following a disaster, you are going to need all of the calories you can get because your stress levels are going to be higher, and you may have to do a lot of things that are now done for you. The goal will be to maintain a healthy body weight and you are going to need foods with caloric substance in order to accomplish that goal.

Here are some other things to consider when thinking about what to grow:

- You're going to want to concentrate your efforts on growing foods that are high in fat and protein.
- You will have to consider how many people you will need to feed, and how much food they will need on a daily basis in order to survive for an extended period.
- Some of the foods you will grow should be able to be stored for an extended period of time, because your growing season may be limited depending on where you live.
- Some foods require larger growing areas than others. How much space do you have? What will you be able to grow in

that space that will give you the largest and best yield for your efforts?

- It is wise to focus on foods that are sustainable, meaning that they are not harmful to the environment in which they are grown and that they do not unnecessarily deplete natural resources.
- You will need to focus your efforts on foods that are appropriate for your climate and the length of your growing season, as well as how easy it is to store them for later use.

Here's a list of foods you should consider growing for your survival needs following disaster:

- **Potatoes** are a great food to grow for your nourishment needs following a catastrophe. They will grow in poor soil, they grow abundantly, they will grow in a wide variety of climates, and they are stuffed with calories. In addition, potatoes will store for a long time without going bad, and depending on your climate, you may be able to grow a double harvest in a single year.

- **Sweet potatoes** are one of the healthiest foods you can eat and they grow easily in many climates. What's more, their leaves are also edible. Sweet potatoes are packed with vitamin A, vitamin C, fiber, and a host of other nutrients that are great for you.

- **Kale** is a leafy green vegetable that is low in calories but high in nutrients, and it is easy to grow. Because of its value as a health food, it may help keep you healthy as you strive to survive out there in an emergency situation.

- **Corn** is easy to grow and easy to store, but it's not high in nutrients. Its value lies in its diversity as a food. Focus on growing grain corn as opposed to sweet corn because you can grind it up and make grits and cornbread with it. Corn has fed people for thousands of years and has thus proven itself as a good source of food.

- **Cabbage** grows relatively easily and is packed with nutrients. In addition, it will store fine in refrigeration or in a root cellar. Fermented cabbage will keep even longer and is said to have healing properties. Cabbage has been known to help with stomach ailments.

- **Beans** need a lot of space in order to grow, but they are a great source of protein, fiber, vitamin B, iron, and potassium. They are also low in fat. There are many varieties of beans from which to choose and they are high in caloric content.

- **Jerusalem artichokes** are hardy root vegetables that grow very easily. Plant the roots in the ground and you can easily access them any time of year provided the ground is not frozen. They will keep indefinitely when raw but you should eat

them within two days after you cook
them.

- **Squashes and pumpkins** are very
  hardy, rich in nutrients, and will store for
  long periods of time at room temperature.
  There is quite a variety of squashes from
  which to choose. Consider canning some
  of your squash to keep for longer periods.

- **Sunflower seeds** are an excellent source
  of protein without the fiber. Grow
  sunflowers in your garden not only
  because of the sunflower seeds, but also
  because the flower will attract bees, which
  will pollinate your garden.

These are just some of the foods that are
considered good candidates for growing in terms
of survival, but they are good ones. Do not be
discouraged about growing a garden. Like
anything else discussed in this book, growing
food requires an investment in time and energy,
but it is well worth it when you reap the rewards
of your labor.

Consider canning some of your food product for bartering purposes as well, as many people will not be prepared and will be craving fresh or canned vegetables and starches following a disaster.

Task Number 13; Procure and Maintain Emergency Supplies in Your Home

Hopefully, if an emergency situation develops in your region, it will not be so severe that you will have to leave your home. Many survivalist experts recommend that you make every effort to remain in surroundings that are familiar, comfortable, and safe for you. Obviously, that is not always possible, and we will address how to prepare for an evacuation from your home if that becomes necessary, but your home is your primary base of operations and it's the best place to be when chaos erupts as long as it remains a safe place to be.

There is strength in numbers in an emergency, and you may want to consider collaborating with your neighbors to create an emergency plan. This is not always possible, because some neighbors may not see the urgency of potential situations and may not buy into a preparatory plan. However, you won't know unless you talk with them about it. Your costs in terms of time, energy, and financing can be greatly reduced if you are working with others to prepare for a disaster. For example, preparation components such as food, water, power, etc. can be split up evenly between parties that agree to participate in the plan.

Whether you have the support of your neighbors or not, there are certain items that you want to keep on hand in your home so that you will be able to sustain yourself and your family in the event of an emergency. The following is a list of items you should consider for your home disaster emergency planning:

Generator: If the power goes out for an hour or two, it's usually not a big deal. The temperature in your home will not be affected too drastically and nothing in your refrigerator will go bad as long as you are careful about keeping the door closed. However, if you lose power for a significant length of time without a backup, you may experience major inconveniences. This is why people purchase generators.

There is a wide variety of options available in today's home generators. It's important to thoroughly research these options because what may work for someone else may not be appropriate for your needs. How much power do you need? How long do you want to prepare for? Should you buy a generator that is very heavy and bulky and powerful, or would it be better to purchase one that is more portable? These are just some of the questions you will need to answer for yourself before you purchase your generator.

Tools: In an emergency situation, it's critical to have the correct tools on hand to help you to complete tasks related to cleanup and survival. Your tool supply should include a hatchet, a rake, a shovel, a broom, a chainsaw, a circular saw, a utility knife, some buckets, a hose, a hammer, a drill, some screwdrivers, a roll of duct tape, some rope, and some fully-charged backup batteries for power tools. In addition, you will also need to store fuel for your generator.

It's worth mentioning here that you should always keep your tools in good working order, and organized in a storage shed or your garage so that you always know where they are. Taking the time to inventory your tools and maintain their ability to perform will save you much aggravation when you need them in a pinch.

Plastic Sheeting: In the event of window breakage, you will need the plastic sheeting to cover the broken windows. Use the duct tape mentioned above to secure the plastic. In addition, plastic sheeting can be used as a makeshift shower curtain, as well as to create an isolated space in your home in case someone comes down with a disease and has to be quarantined in some fashion. Plastic sheeting can also be used to collect rainwater.

Durable Clothing: You are likely to have plenty of clothing on hand in your home, but make sure each person has long pants, long sleeved shirts, wool socks, a rain jacket or poncho, and a pair of sturdy shoes or boots to wear in the event of a disaster. You are also going to want to make sure that each person has a pair of work gloves in order to protect their hands when debris has to be moved or when other similar manual labor has to be done.

If you reside in a cold climate, you should also make sure that everyone in your home has a hat, a scarf, and a heavy coat to protect themselves from the harsh elements of winter.

Food: Keep an emergency supply designated for disasters in a secure and dry place. You will want to store nonperishable foods, such as canned and dried products, enough to sustain you and your family for at least three days. If you have pets, make sure you cover their needs in terms of nourishment as well. If you have not done so already, please be sure and read the section on growing food for survival that appears previously in this chapter.

Water: Store at least one gallon per day for each person living in your home. In addition, store some bleach and a medicine dropper for water sanitization purposes. Make sure you have water stored for your pets, as well, if you have them.

Keep in mind that your plumbing may fail in the event of an emergency, and you may consider keeping a supply of water on hand to use for hygienic purposes.

Tools for Dining: These would include a manual can opener and plastic cups, plates, and utensils. Plastic dinnerware is recommended because water may be scarce and it may be easier to simply dispose of your dinnerware following use than it would be to wash and reuse it.

Illumination: Portable camping lanterns are ideal for when the power goes down, but choose the battery-charged model as opposed to a propane or butane-fueled lantern because it's safer. In addition, make sure you have flashlights. Candles are not only good sources for illumination, but they are also heat and ignition sources. Make sure you have backup batteries for your flashlights and lanterns. In addition, you will need a fuel source for your candles, such as matches or lighters.

NOAA Weather Radio: Your weather radio will help keep you informed of conditions outside of your home. Consider purchasing one that can be hand-cranked as opposed to one that operates off of batteries.

Fire Extinguisher: A lot of families have fire extinguishers in their homes, but most of them probably have no idea how to use it in the event of a fire. Don't be caught off-guard in an emergency: take that fire extinguisher out in the backyard and learn how to use it well before you need it. Remember: it's all about preparation.

Dust Masks: Dust masks will serve to offer your lungs some protection if the air has become unsafe due to damage around you. Keep enough on hand so that you have fresh ones daily if needed.

First Aid Kit: There are plenty of standard pre-packaged first aid kits out on the market, but you may want to consider packing your own. Designing your own first aid kit allows you to put what you know you will need in it, and also gives you the opportunity to become knowledgeable about its contents. Make sure you research what you will need, though. In addition, purchase a first aid manual and keep it with your first aid kit.

Medication: It is always wise to make sure you have enough medication on hand for at least three days, but in an emergency situation it is critical.

Hygienic Supplies: Hygiene is important in any situation, and especially in critical situations. Make sure you have soap, disinfectant, hand sanitizer, toilet paper, wet napkins, and paper towels, as well as a bucket to use as a toilet in case the plumbing shuts down.

Task Number 14: Shut Services Down if Necessary

While your home may be the safest place for you and your family in the event of a disaster, you may have to perform a few tasks in order to keep it way depending on the nature of the emergency. If you have natural gas in your home, it is highly recommended that you check to make sure your source is secure. If you smell gas, hear gas escaping, or see a broken gas line or suspect a leak for some other reason, shut off the gas. If you don't know how to shut off the gas source in your home, consult your gas company as soon as possible to obtain instructions. Then, place the instructions along with a wrench and a flashlight in an area specifically designated for them.

A disaster may break exterior water lines, and that may allow contaminated water to enter your home. In order to shut off the water line that feeds your home, simply locate and shut down the main water valve in your home. Of course, you should learn where that water valve is today if you don't know where it is.

Flooding can cause real havoc to your electrical system in your home. Be sure to shut off the electricity if you expect a flood. If there is water already in your basement, do not go near the electrical panel.

Task Number 15: Prepare Your Automobile

We take so much in life for granted and most of us never even think about being stranded in our cars. But it happens all of the time. There are numerous accounts of people getting stranded in their cars during snowstorms and then being found dead days later. Be prepared. Keep an emergency kit in every car with basic supplies to sustain you in the event of an emergency. Here's a list of what you should consider for your kit:

Local Maps and a Road Atlas: With today's technology, most people think that they are covered in terms of navigation by their GPS device. However, if the satellites or the electrical grid collapse, you will be out of luck unless you have some good old paper maps. Keep them in your kit. You may never need them, but always remember that we are preparing for events that many of us cannot even imagine.

Writing Supplies: If you decide to venture out away from your vehicle during an emergency, you are going to want to leave a note of some sort in the car telling potential rescuers where you are, or which way you are headed. Keep a notepad and some pens and pencils in your kit for this purpose.

Food: Keep some nuts, dried fruit, cookies, and energy bars in your kit in order to sustain you if you are stranded for a while.

Water: Two gallons will sustain you for two days, or you and a passenger for one day. If necessary, you can stretch your supply a bit as well.

Blankets or Sleeping Bag: These will help you retain body heat if necessary.

Hygienic Supplies: Keep some toilet paper, hand sanitizer, wet napkins, and trash bags on hand in order to keep yourself and your car tidy in the event of an emergency.

Duct Tape: This is so versatile and can assist you with glass breakage, as well as temporary hose repair. In addition, you can twist a long piece of it into a rope and use it to tow your car if necessary.

Cellphone Car Charger: This is a must in an emergency situation. Don't leave home without a way to charge your cellphone on the fly. Batteries don't last forever.

Extra Clothing: Keep a sweater or fleece in your kit, as well as raingear and sturdy shoes. Depending on the climate, you may want to keep gloves, a scarf, and a hat on hand as well.

First-Aid Kit: Your portable first-aid kit should include bandages, an antibiotic ointment, an antiseptic, ibuprofen or aspirin, an antidiarrheal, and some medical tape.

Tools: A good sturdy multi-tool, a powerful flashlight, and a utility knife are great to have on hand to assist you in the event of an emergency.

Fire Extinguisher: Make sure you know how to use your fire extinguisher before you actually need it.

Jumper Cables: These are an absolute necessity. Again, make sure you know how to use them before you need them. Using jumper cables incorrectly can do serious damage to either cars' electrical systems.

Light Sticks or Roadside Flares: Use these to warn drivers that you are where you are, for safety and for rescue purposes.

Towline: This can be used for towing a car out of a ditch or other hazardous location.

Task Number 16: Prepare Your Bug-Out Bags

A bug-out bag is a kit you will prepare that will allow you to "bug out," or evacuate quickly following a disaster. Your bug-out bag will contain everything you will need in order to survive for a seventy-two-hour period.

The contents of your bug-out bag may vary depending on where you live and your own specific needs, but every bug-out bag should at least contain the following items:

- **The Bugout-Bag Itself:** It is highly advisable to purchase your bug-out bag after you procure all of the items you plan to put into it.

- **Water:** For drinking purposes, you are going to need one liter minimum per person per day. Ideally, you will need a bit more for cleaning purposes. In addition, your bug-out bag should contain some water bottles or canteens, as well as some water purification tablets.

- **Food / Food Preparation Gear:** In considering what food to include in your bug-out bag, it is smart to try out various foods to make sure you can actually eat whatever you choose to include. Not all survival food is created equally, but I can assure you that with a bit of research, you will find something that appeals to you.

Have at least three protein bars on hand. Protein helps you build and maintain muscle mass and also feeds your red blood cells, which will help wounds heal in a timely manner.

It's also a wise idea to have three energy bars in your bag as well. Energy bars typically contain concentrated carbohydrates.

MREs (Meals Ready to Eat) are dehydrated meals designed by the United States military to sustain troops when they are out in places without cooking facilities. Many MREs are self-heating, and many are sold in packages of three, which is the number recommended for your bug-out bag.

A portable stove is a good item to have in your bug-out bag, as well as a metal cooking pot, a spork, a can opener, a metal cup, a pot scrubber, and some stove fuel.

- **Clothing:** The clothing you include in your bug-out bag will be largely dependent on your own body type, level of fitness, and your tolerance, but the goal of your clothing should be to maintain your body at a healthy body temperature. In addition, you will need to consider the climate and the season for your region, and for that reason the clothing in your bag should be re-evaluated as the seasons change.

Ideally, you will want to include at least two sets of clothing. While it's fairly tolerable to wear soiled clothes for a short period of time, you are going to be very uncomfortable if your clothes get wet and you will risk hypothermia as well.
Your clothing list should include:

- One lightweight long sleeve shirt;
- One pair zip-off pants;
- Underwear / undershirts (two minimum)
- Three pair wool socks
- Fleece jacket (medium weight)
- Brimmed hat
- Utility gloves
- Poncho / rain gear

- **Shelter and Bedding:** Do your research and look for lightweight materials in this category. Include a high-quality sleeping bag and a tent, as well as a tarp and a ground pad. And, depending on the time of year, it might be a good idea to include a wool blanket as well.

- **Fire Starters:** Fire is essential for warmth and for cooking when disaster strikes and it pays to have redundant sources of ignition in your bug-out bag. As most anyone who has ever been camping knows, it's not always easy to start a fire and the more tools you have to help you, the better.

  For this reason, pack at least three ignition sources, three tinder bundles, and waterproof storage in which to keep your fire starters.

- **First Aid:** There are many pre-packaged first-aid kits on the market, but it is best to build your own because conserving space in your bug-out bag is a priority, and a pre-packaged first aid kit is most likely going to contain items you are not likely to need. In addition, if you take the time to pack your own first aid kit, you are going to know exactly what it contains in the event that you need to turn to it as part of your survival.

The Red Cross recommends that you keep all medications in your first-aid kit, as well as emergency phone numbers and any other items recommended by your healthcare provider. You should also check your first-aid kit regularly to make sure everything is still in place, and to replace any items that have been used or removed. You should also check expirations dates on all items that have them and replace any items that are past their date.

- **Cleansing Kit**: Things may get pretty gritty out there on your evacuation route and it is best to be prepared with some items to conduct a quick cleanup when necessary. Each bug-out bag should have some hand sanitizer in it, as well as some all-purpose concentrated camp soap. In addition, pack some wet napkins, a small towel, a small mirror (that you can use to see yourself, and to signal a plane or something if need be), and two rolls of travel toilet paper.

- **Tools:** Obviously, there won't be room in your bug-out bag for your toolbox, but you will be amazed what can be packed into a small multi-tool that folds up into a neat little package. Leatherman and Swiss Army are just two companies that manufacture and distribute such products and they usually come with a warranty that covers breakage. A good multi-tool will contain at least one knife, one screwdriver, one Phillips screwdriver, pliers, and a can / bottle opener.

The other tool you will need to have is a good sturdy survival knife. Again, there are many good brands out there. Remember that you get what you pay for, and because your survival may depend on the quality, get one with a strong blade and a handle with a comfortable grip.

- **Illumination:** It's going to get dark out there if the power goes out and the moon is not out, so you're going to have to be prepared to light your way. LED headlamps are great tools and every bug-out bag should have one. Wearing one of these will allow you to see what you are doing while keeping your hands free. In addition, keep a small penlight on your keychain, and pack a larger flashlight as well.

Pack at least three emergency survival candles. These are slow burning candles that will last for hours and have the ability to provide light in a room, extra heat, and a cooking source. It's also easier to light a larger fire from a candle than it is from a lighter or a match.

- **Communication Equipment:** Obviously, you are going to want to pack a cell phone in your bug-out bag. This is because the phone you usually carry around with you may not be accessible in an emergency. Purchase a wireless prepaid phone and stick it in your bag along with a few prepaid cards.

We all take electricity for granted, and while we may occasionally be inconvenienced when we are out and have to watch our cell phone battery slowly run down, we are comforted by the knowledge that we are not far from an outlet and a charger.

Forget all of that when the grid goes down. For that reason, you are going to need a backup charger that is powered by batteries, a hand crank, or both. Power chargers available today are truly versatile and many have illumination capabilities, as well as radios. Prices range from about $70 to $200. Most are able to charge a cell phone up to three times before they have to be repowered.

If your portable charger does not contain an emergency radio, you should purchase one separately and stick it in your bag. Like portable chargers, many come with various features such as built-in flashlights and built-in speaker systems instead of headphone jacks. Some run strictly on batteries while others have AC power adapters you can use when power is available. Whichever you choose, make sure it is able to accept emergency alert signals from either the "Public Alert" system or the "NOAA NWR All Hazards" system, preferably both.

Another useful tool in regards to communications to have in your bag is a heavy-duty charging cable. While the one that came with your phone is great for home use, the one you take out on the road during an emergency situation may get beat up or exposed to the elements. For that reason, it's smart to consider investing in a third-party cable that is designed for heavy-duty use.

Two other communications items you will need are an emergency whistle, and a small mirror. Voices, even yelling voices, will only carry so far, and may not help you if you need to get the attention of potential rescuers from a distance. A good loud whistle, though, has the potential to get people's attention, as does the glare from a mirror that is reflecting the sun toward them.

- **Currency:** No one can predict what will be accepted as currency in the event of a disaster, but one can reasonably assume that cold hard cash will still work, at least in the short term. For that reason, you need to have at least $500 in small bills in your bug-out bag. Small bills are recommended because those you encounter may not be in a position to make change. If you can swing a larger amount to pack away, by all means do it, but $500 should carry you through the first seventy-two hours of an emergency.

  It's also wise to keep a stash of quarters in your bag so that you can use them in vending machines or pay phones if you need to do so.

Finally, many survivalist experts recommend that you keep several gold and /or silver coins on hand in the event that paper currency becomes obsolete. This is unlikely in most circumstances, but one never knows what will happen, right? Gold and silver have been used for currency or for bartering purposes for hundreds of years and have traditionally been viewed as valuable. Of course, like paper currency, no one can predict with one hundred percent accuracy that gold and silver will hold its value in the future, but my guess is that if you find yourself needing something in a crunch if and when the world goes totally crazy, chances are that gold and silver may be more palatable to the person holding what you need than paper money.

- **Navigation:** With today's technology, many of us have become very reliant on our GPS (which stands for "global positioning system, by the way) devices to get us from point A to point B. GPS devices rely on electricity and satellites in order to provide us with accurate information to relay to us. In the event of an electrical or satellite failure, though, you are going to have to revert to older methods.

Your bug-out bag should contain maps of the general area in which you live, as well as maps that cover the route you plan on using in case you need to evacuate. Your bag should also contain a reliable compass that you will use along with your maps to help you find your way around when the GPS no longer works. These tools are going to be useless to you, though, unless you know how to use them. Take the time now to learn how to read your maps and to use your compass so that you do not have to figure it out after the disaster is upon you. There are plenty of books and websites that will provide you with the information you need in order to become proficient in reading maps and using a compass.

- **Self Defense:** Let's face it: no one wants to really think about being threatened by other people when they are out there trying to take care of themselves or their family during and following a disaster, but the reality is that when supplies necessary for human survival get scarce, people may resort to desperate behaviors in order to get what they need. For that reason, you need to take measures to protect yourself and your family from predators that may want what you have so thoughtfully taken the time to prepare for the disaster you are facing.

There are various opinions about just what to include in your bug-out bag in terms of self-protection, but one of the less controversial items to include is pepper spray, particularly if you are not going to carry a firearm. Pepper spray can be purchased very easily on the Internet and in retail stores that feature camping equipment. Make sure you do your research because not all pepper spray devices are created equally. Look for one that disperses the spray in a cone spray as opposed to one that shoots out the product in a straight line. In addition, your pepper spray device should fit comfortably in your hand and in your pocket, and you should practice using it well before you need to use it in an emergency situation.

Not everyone reading this has ever used a firearm before, but it's worth considering getting trained with firearms and purchasing one that suits your needs at some point. One never knows what can happen in this world, and an EMP or similar catastrophic event has the potential to turn our society into complete anarchy very quickly.

By the way, as I write this, our rights guaranteed to us by virtue of the Second Amendment of the United States Constitution are under attack by those who believe that law-abiding citizens should not be allowed to have firearms. While it is definitely fact that there are a lot of people out there that should definitely not have guns, some would argue that the only way for law-abiding folks to protect themselves, particularly in a chaotic situation following a natural disaster, is to have weapons to help them protect themselves, their loved ones, and their property. The controversy regarding the Second Amendment and the right to bear arms is not going away any time soon, but it may be best to consider purchasing a gun now, as opposed to later, because it may be too late someday.

There are many options for firearms, but for purposes of this discussion, you should be well-trained on any weapon you choose. Remember, this book is all about preparation and it would not be smart to simply purchase a weapon for your bug-out bag and not learn how to properly load it, clean it, and shoot it. Know your weapon as well as you possibly can and teach yourself to use it safely and accurately.

A pistol may be a good choice because it is compact and easily stored, but the problem with a pistol is similar to the problem discussed above with some pepper spray devices: you have to be a very good marksman in order to bring down your target. A shotgun, alternatively, shoots its ammunition with a wider spray, but it is bulkier thus more difficult to maneuver in tight quarters. You are going to have to carefully weigh your options and then make the appropriate choice for you.

Whatever firearm you choose, make sure you have ammunition as well.

Chapter 6: Be Alert

Task Number 17: Be Situationally Aware

I touched upon the importance of being aware of your surroundings when you are out and about earlier in this book, but it is worth addressing the topic of situational awareness in more detail. Increasingly, incidents have occurred across the world that have caught innocent people totally off guard and have resulted in severe injury and loss of life. Sadly, we can reasonably predict that these sort of events may continue indefinitely, which means it is extremely important to pay close attention to the environments in which we may find ourselves.

The following tips are not offered with the suggestion that you meander around the planet in a constant state of paranoia, but we are suggesting that a healthy amount of situational awareness may keep you safe in an emergency.

Tip #1: Travel Carefully

When you are in transit, whether you are on foot or in or on a vehicle, be aware of the environment through which you are moving and all of its potential hazards. If you are walking, minimize your risk of injury by paying attention to your foot placement, as well as potential obstacles in front and to the sides of you. If you are behind the wheel of an automobile or on a bicycle or motorcycle, allow enough distance between you and other vehicles in order to minimize risk of collision. Always keep your focus on the path in front of you. Do not allow yourself to be distracted by cellphone calls or texts, and do not compromise your focus by trying to eat, or read the newspaper, or apply makeup. To summarize this point, travel deliberately and with total focus on your mission to get from point A to point B as safely as possible.

Tip #2: Use Your Senses to Engage Your Environment

Wherever you are, use your eyes, ears, and nose to detect irregularities in your environment. Pay particular attention to loud noises that occur suddenly, and to odors that may signal a gas leak. Periodically scan the environment to see if anything or anyone appears to be out of place or acting strangely. Make sure that you are aware of where the exits are in a room and always pay attention to who is entering the building.

Tip #3: Be Aware of What is Behind You

It is entirely natural to give the majority of your attention to what is going on in front of you, but people who are situationally aware also pay attention to what is going on behind them. It's not a great idea to wear ear buds as you are walking down the street because you may need your ears to hear someone sneaking up behind you. As you walk, periodically turn your head and take note of anyone that may be following behind you. Granted, most times other people around you will mean you no harm, but it is always much better to be safe than sorry.

Tip #4: Be Attentive to the Mood

Be aware of people's body language and how and what they are communicating to those around them. It's fairly easy to tell when someone around you is agitated or upset, and it's best to move away from situations where attitudes like that exist even if nothing becomes of it. Of course, there may be times when you may be forced to intervene, but make sure you do it in a way that minimizes physical risk to anyone in the immediate area.

Tip #5: Trust Your Instincts

Sometimes you may be out and about and just get a feeling that the environment is not safe for whatever reason. It's always prudent to pay attention to your instincts, particularly if they have served you well in the past. At the very least, take time to try and figure out what is making you uncomfortable before you decide to either go with the feeling or discount it. If you try and place a thought with the feeling, you may be able to pinpoint the source of your discomfort and then make a more focused decision about how to respond.

Conclusion

Hopefully, this book has enlightened your perspective on potential disasters that could occur and how to go about preparing for them. As stated previously, there are plenty of people all over the world who consider disaster preparation to be important enough to devote a significant deal of time, energy, and money toward the mission. We leave you with a few quotes to inspire you toward action:

"It wasn't raining when Noah built the ark." - Howard Ruff

"Despair is most often the offspring of ill-preparedness." - Don Williams, Jr.

"Preparation through education is less costly than learning through tragedy." - Max Mayfield, Director, National Hurricane Center